Discovering Gods' Purpose
and
Plan for Your Life

Rev. Deborah Warren

Order this book online at www.trafford.com
or email orders@trafford.com

Most Trafford titles are also available at major online book retailers.

Printed in the United States of America.

ISBN: 978-1-4669-5980-4 (sc)
ISBN: 978-1-4669-5981-1 (e)

Trafford rev. 01/22/2013

 www.trafford.com

North America & international
toll-free: 1 888 232 4444 (USA & Canada)
phone: 250 383 6864 ♦ fax: 812 355 4082

Content

Subject	Page

Introduction...7

Chapter 1

The Case for Discovery..10

Chapter 2

The Valleys of Life...12

Decision

Suffering

Affliction

Lack or Famine

Judgment

Shadow of Death

Chapter 3

The Process of Fulfilling God's Purpose and Plan for Your Life 18

Salvation
Principles of Salvation
Salvation Involves Our Will or Volition

Chapter 4

Forgiveness v/s Unforgiveness 24

Chapter 5

Making Christ King...28

Subject	Page

Chapter 6

Service...31

Chapter 7

Passion as it Relates to Purpose.......................................34

Chapter 8

Stewardship...38

Chapter 9

Suffering...41

Chapter 10

Moving to the Next Era of Divine Purpose..............................44

Chapter 11

Pick Up Your Shield and Trust the Captain 48

Chapter 12

Spiritual Armor and Weapons of Warfare 51

Chapter 13

Spiritual Gifts..54

Review

Bibliographical References

Introduction

Not taking anything for granted, as we often do, by assuming that all those that we meet have come to the revelatory truth of and knowledge of the true and living God, who created heaven, the earth, the universe, the fowl of the air, the fish of the sea, the creatures and creeping things on the earth, the angels in heaven including Lucifer (the devil or Satan as we call or know him).

This living God also made man, both male and female in His image, and gave them dominion over the earth, which includes the fish of the sea, the fowl of the air, the cattle, and every creeping thing that creeps on the earth.

As you study Gods word you will become familiar with what is known as the Godhead, which includes God the Father in creation, God the Son in redemption, and God the Holy Spirit in comfort (or the comforter).

Because of disobedience sin came into the world. However this disobedience did not begin on earth but actually began in heaven with the sin of pride and envy. Where Lucifer (Satan or the devil as we know him) also called the son of the morning, declared in four "I will" statements that he would take Gods' place. Isaiah 14: 13-14 which states "For thou hast said in thine heart, I will ascend into heaven, I will exalt my throne above the stars of God, I will sit also upon the mount of the congregation, in the sides of the north; I will ascend above the heights of the clouds; I will be like the most High," And was cast out of heaven. (Luke 10:18 KJV.)

Now God planted a garden eastward of Eden, and He took man and placed him in the garden, which we call the Garden of Eden, that he should dress it and keep it. God gave man a commandment that of every tree of this garden he could freely eat; but of the tree of knowledge of good and evil, he could not eat. God even told man of the consequences of eating of this tree. That in the day that he would eat of this tree, he would surely die.

Earlier we spoke of Lucifer or the devil, or Satan as we know him, being cast out of heaven was also on the earth, and being one of the most cunning creatures on earth, in the form of the serpent, came to the woman which God had formed for the man help meet, to deceive her, by bringing up what God had said in His commandment about the forbidden tree in the midst of the Garden of Eden, causing the same sin that caused him to be cast out of heaven in the first place, the sin of pride, to be brought to earth by mans' disobedience.

Chapter 1

The
Case
For

Discovery

The Case for Discovery

Let's take a journey. On this journey there are some hidden treasures to be found. We'll call them life's hidden nuggets.

There is clothing to be put on and to take off. We'll call this clothing the old nature the new nature and God's armor.

There are people on this journey, some have always been there, and we'll call them family. We didn't choose them we were born into this group. And then there are friends, associates, husbands, wives, all to some extent our choice. And then there are our enemies or adversaries, and of course there are those who have rule over us, for instance pastors, teachers, employers, government.

Then we come to the eras of life in which we travel, our ups, our downs, our in betweens, our joys, our disappointments, our mountain top and valley experiences, and speaking of valleys, these are many and some of them are growth experiences, namely (1) the valley of decision, (2) the valley of judgment, (3) the valley of suffering, (4) the valley of affliction, (5) the valley of lack or famine, and (6) the valley of the shadow of death. In this life we will go through one or more of these either by choice or as a growth experience. However we must not set up camp in these valleys for we will not remain there. On each side of the valley there are mountains of victory, and we endure the valley either alone or with God's help, the choice is ours, just remember that no man is an island and no man stands alone, we need help in every area of our lives. God will not give nor share His glory with another (Isaiah 42:8) yet He chose to give us His best. He gave His only begotten Son, Jesus the Christ, as the perpetuation for the reconciliation of man back to God the Father through the shedding of His blood on the cross on a hill called Calvary, for the law said without the shedding of blood there is no remission of man's sin (Hebrews 10:22).

There is life in the shed blood of Jesus Christ. This brings us right back to our choice. I chose life and victory through the shed blood of Jesus Christ. You must also choose as no one can make that choice for you. My encouragement to you is that you will choose life and victory in Jesus Christ, for He, Himself states that "I am the way, the truth, and the life, no man comes to the Father except by me" (John 14:6). In our choice we must first seek the Kingdom of God and His righteousness, and God's Word says that all these things will be added. We often think of the Kingdom of God as a place but it is really God's way of doing things. The Kingdom of Heaven on the other hand is a place.

Chapter 2

The
Valleys
of
Life

The Valleys of Life

The Valley of Decision

First of all what exactly is a decision. A working definition would be the determination to follow a course of action. Since we are calling it a valley, literally a valley is a depression in land between hills or mountains. And thus we must determine which route or course of action to take while at this fork in the road of our journey. To accept or reject the Kingdom of God (God's way of doing things) in this valley either we have already accepted the gift that God has already given to us when He gave His Son, and if not this is the time to do so. Remember Jesus Christ is the door to the Kingdom of God, and to enter in we must accept Him in His fullness, as revealed to us, Father in creation, Son in redemption, and Holy Spirit in Comfort. In order to do this we must first believe that God exist and is a rewarder of them that diligently seek Him, (Hebrews 11:6) and not just a higher being, or just the man upstairs, but the creator of all things including you and I. To seek means to look into or to search for. What are you searching or seeking for? Are you seeking for someone that you can place your trust or faith in? Life as it has proved that it cannot be man, whether he has put on his new clothing (the new nature) or is still wearing his/her old clothing (the old nature). In Exodus chapter 3 God said in answering Moses "I Am That I AM". This answered for Moses who shall I say sent me to the children of Israel. But to me it says I am whatever I need him to be, peace, a provider, a lawyer, joy, a healer, a friend, father, mother, sister, brother, shelter in a storm, an advocate, just to name a few. The decision is yours alone. When you make your decision please understand that this decision will affect the rest of your life, because you will be choosing life or death. Which will you be, a dead man or woman walking in sin, or alive in Christ Jesus? I exhort you to choose life.

The Valley of Suffering

If we name the name of Jesus the Christ, If we are sold out to Jesus the Christ, If you choose to live a holy and righteous life, sanctified justified and set aside, as the Word of God says come out from among them. If you seek the kingdom of God (God's way of doing things) and its righteousness to lay hold of the commanded blessings therein, you will suffer, not for evil but for righteousness. It is all in the plan that God has for your life. A working definition of suffering is to endure pain, or distress unto death Jeremiah 29:11 states; "For I know the thoughts (plans) that I think toward you, says the Lord, thoughts of peace, and not of evil, to give you a future and a hope".

We must rejoice when we suffer for righteous sake, because you are in a good place, you are having a head on collision with Satan and the flesh. Satan hates you just as much as he hated Jesus. The Holy Spirit will teach you how to suffer. So we will have trials, and persecutions, just as Jesus did when He walked on the earth. 1 Peter 4:12-14 says "Beloved, do not think it strange concerning the fiery trials which is to try you, as though some strange thing happened to you: but rejoice to the extent that you partake of Christ's sufferings, that when His glory is revealed, you may also be glad with exceeding joy. If you are reproached for the name of Christ, blessed are you, for the Spirit of glory and of God rests upon you. On their part He is blasphemed, but on your part He is glorified."

Before we came into the revelation, of the truth, of the true and living God, and His Son Jesus, the Christ whose blood was shed on the cross at Calvary. We suffered with no assurance in anything solid but in sinking sand as a foundation to live by. But God's word says in the book of Hebrew

"For we know Him that said, Vengeance is mine, I will repay, says the Lord. And again, The Lord will judge His people. It is a fearful thing to fall into the hands of the living God. But recall the former days in which, after you were illuminated, you endured great struggle with sufferings:" Hebrews 10:30-32.

"Therefore do not cast away your confidence, which has great reward. For you have need of endurance, so that after you have done the will of God, you may receive the promise." Hebrews 10:35-36.

The Valley of Affliction

A working definition of an affliction is the endurance of hardships and or trials, infirmities, disabilities and limitations. You will have afflictions if you place your trust in God and depend on Him in every area of your life. "Many are the afflictions of the righteous, but the Lord delivered him out of them all." (Psalms 34:19)

In the natural or the physical realm we will find that there are many obstacles that we will go through, whether sickness, financial difficulties, diseases, accidents, wounds, spiritual, physical and emotional. Our choices have a lot to do with many of the afflictions that may attach themselves to us. Some may also be spiritual. Jesus says take my yoke upon you and learn of me for my yoke is easy and my burdens are light. In order to take on the yoke of Jesus, we must not only accept Him as savior, but also allow Him to be lord of our lives. Then we can cast our cares upon Him for He cares for us, and there is nothing or no problem or trouble to big for Him to handle. He neither sleeps nor slumbers and where He guides, He also provides. Often times afflictions are designed to cause us to seek the face of God, to bring us back to Him after our moving away from Him, to humble us, or to test us. Many times we rebel and just simply refuse to obey God's word, His prophets or the shepherds (pastors) who have been given charge over our lives out of pride and deliberate sin. We must also remember that when we get lifted up in pride (the "I" syndrome) God will humble us, or bring us back down where we should be under Him. And there are times that our faith is tested.

The Valley of Lack or Famine

To look at this valley lets get a working definition of lack and of famine. Lack is when something is still needed or there is not enough of what is needed, and famine is an extreme scarcity of what is needed. These can be in any area of our lives. Examples would be food, finances, etc. They can come under the categories of physical (natural) or Spiritual. Famine has several causes, Sin (Ezek.14: 12-13), punishment (2 King 8:1), siege (2 King 6:25), or weather (Ex.9: 23) they can often be devastating, severe, destructive, and last long periods of time. Lack on the other hand can be subject to food (2 Sam.3: 29), physical needs (2 Cor.11: 9), possessions (1 Sam. 30:19), services to others (Phil.2: 30), wisdom (James 1:5), and commitments (Luke 18:22).

Times of famine and lack affect every area of our lives, when it exists. During these times our attitude, our reaction, and our source, that thing we depend on to relieve the distress we are under during these times. Our attitude will affect how we react to the circumstances we are under. Our source will affect the stressfulness of the circumstances, and the determination of the outcome of the situation. Who or what is your source? Who or what supplies your daily needs? If you have not accepted Jesus Christ as lord and savior of your life, then you are your only source or maybe Satan, because you have chosen to reject the gift that God has given to man to reconcile man back to the Himself. God's word says to seek the Kingdom of God and its righteousness, and all these things will be added to you. Exactly what does this mean? It means to seek or search out God's way of doing things in other words the method God uses to further the His Kingdom, after applying His method to your life, all the other material as well as spiritual things will be added. God is the owner, and provider of all things. Jesus the Son of God states Himself "I am the way, the truth, and the life, no one comes to the Father except by me" (John 14:6). God gave his only Son that whosoever believes in Him will not perish but will have in turn everlasting life. (John 3:16) Please understand that whatever your choice during famine and lack, both the unregenerate and the regenerated are affected in this world. God rains upon the just as well as the unjust. God has promised to never leave nor forsake us, and to provide all of our needs according to His riches in glory through Christ Jesus. When we choose to accept Jesus as our savoir, and make Him lord of our lives, these afflictions are easier to go through. And through has an end. Therefore we are able to cast our cares on Him, because He cares for us.

The Valley of Judgment

Understand that God is a good God, and that yes He knows our heart and our thoughts before we even think them. Why? Because He, Himself is the manufacturer of man. He is our creator. He made man in His image and being made in the image of God, God has a will, and so He gave man a will. He could have made us as robots to worship, praise, and obey his laws, statues, and commandments with no choice. He chose to allow us to choose to worship, praise, and obey His word, statues, laws, and commandments. We fall into the valley of judgment when we choose to reject and not diligently heed God's Word. When we do this we bring about many of God's curses upon our lives as those stated in Deuteronomy 28:15-68. I will only name a few of them you can read them for yourself. "But it shall come to pass, if thou wilt not hearken unto the voice of thy God, to observe to do all His statues which I command you this day; that all these curses shall come upon thee, and overtake thee: Cursed shalt thou be in the city and cursed shalt thou be in the field. Cursed shall be thy basket and thy store. Cursed shall be the fruit of thy body, and the fruit of thy land, the increase of thy kine, and the flocks of thy sheep. Cursed shalt thou be when thou comest in, and cursed shalt thou be when thou goest out. The Lord shall send upon thee cursing, vexation, and rebuke, in all that thou settest thou hands to do, until thou be destroyed, and until thou perish quickly, because of thou wickedness of thy doings, whereby thou hast forsaken me. Thou shall betroth (marry) a wife and another man/woman shall lie with her/him: thou shall build a house and shall not dwell therein; thou shall plant a vineyard (garden) and shalt not gather the fruit or vegetables from it. And thy life shall hang in doubt before thee; and thou shalt fear day and night, and shalt have no assurance of thy life. So understand that we have a choice to live under the curse of disobedience

14

or to live in the commanded blessings of God our father. In the end God Himself will be the ultimate judge. I would not want to live here on earth in hell and under the curses of judgment only to be judged by God, and live forever in hell. Hell is a real place set-aside for Satan his children and followers.

The Valley of the Shadow of Death

When we think of death, we readily think of dying, as death is defined as the cessation of life. This can be both physical and spiritual. Physical death is the separation of the spirit from the physical body. And spiritual death is separation spiritually from God the father. Now lets look at shadow, a working definition of shadow is a reflection of a form or a delusive image or semblance, anything unreal or unsubstantial, in this case the reflection of death. A reflection in itself cannot hurt you, but can cause you to hurt yourself. The twenty-third Psalms speaks of walking through the valley of the shadow of death and not being afraid. There is a reason for no fear in this instance. Fear is having faith in the wrong set of realities. In this instance we must know who and what we are trusting in, self, Satan or God. Fear on the other hand is false evidence appearing real, in other words anxiety caused by approaching danger. The danger in this case is not real. It is your perception that makes it appear to be real and causes you to be anxious. Fear is a spirit, which was not given by God our father. 2 Timothy 1:7 states "God has not given us a spirit of fear; but of power, and of love, and of a sound mind." The psalm goes on to say, "For thou art with me". God has promised that He would never leave not forsake us. (Hebrews 13:5, 1Samuel 12:22,) During this era of time in our lives, there may be silence from God or what we call a dead zone, delayed answers to prayers as in Daniel 10: 11-15, where as the answer to Daniels's prayer and supplications were held up by demonic forces (the prince of Persia which is a territorial demon) for twenty one days, devastating illnesses, as in Job 3:3-5 which says, "Let the day perish wherein I was born, and the night in which it was said, There is a man child conceived. Let that day be darkness; let not God regard it from above, neither let the light shine upon it. Let darkness and the shadow of death stain it; let a cloud dwell upon it; let the blackness of the day terrify it." Job was going through a valley of the shadow of death.

This valley can be quite depressing at times especially if you have no one that you can depend on for your needs, or to talk to and get answers from for your life. These are those times, which try man's very soul. What is the state of your soul right now? Who speaks into your life, and what happens when they are not available? What do you do when the phone calls stop? What do you do when there is no encouragement from anyone? The Bible says that David encouraged himself. Who is praying for you? All that you hear is quietness. Life goes on for everyone else. There is no word to apply to this area of your life coming from anyone. What do you do?

You have just entered a valley of the shadow of death. If you have never been in a valley of the shadow of death, keep living. Whether saint or sinner, regenerated, or un-regenerated you will travel through the valley of the shadow of death. This is not a time to retreat but a time to sincerely seek God's face and not His hand concerning your situation. For God will perfect that which concerns you, if you have accepted His original gift. Matthew 11:29-30 says "Take my yoke up you, and learn of me; for I am meek and lowly of heart: and you shall rest unto your souls. For my yoke is easy and my burdens are light". During your journey through this valley of the shadow of death, you will need your burdens not just to be light but often lifted off of your shoulders.

For this is a time in life where many in the church are so busy doing ministry to those on the outside the walls that we often forget that we need to be ministered to also. And during these times we need it most. During each of our valleys experiences, understand that because of our need, we may get hurt by what is called friendly fire, and no one knows you have even been hurt.

So whom do you turn to when there is no one else to turn to? Who do you talk to when nobody wants to listen? Who do you lean on when there is no foundation stable? This will depend on your position whether in Christ of not. Since the world's way of doing things is as sinking sand, the only stable foundation is that of Jesus Christ. This valley will also take you into the valley of decision, as you may have to make some decisions, and discern whether this valley is a shadow or if it is the real thing.

Remember your decision will affect the rest of your life from this point on. Understand we never remain in the valleys. They were not designed for living life just for growing and moving to the end of our journey. They are designed to travel through.

Chapter 3

The Process of Fulfilling God's

Plan & Purpose

For Your

Life

The Process of Fulfilling God's Purpose and Plan for Your Life

Salvation + Spiritual Growth = Transformation into His Likeness

Salvation
The total work of God in affecting a right relationship between mankind and Himself

Romans 10:9-10 "That if thou should confess with thy mouth the Lord Jesus, and shall believe in thine heart that God has raised him from the dead, thou shalt be saved. For with the heart man believeth unto righteousness; and with the mouth confession is made unto salvation." (KJV)

1 John 3: 1-3 "How great is the love the Father has lavished on us, that we should be called the children of God! And that is what we are! The reason the world does not know us is that it did not know Him. Dear friends now we are children of God, and what we will be has not yet been made known. But we know that when He appears we shall be like Him, for we shall see Him as He is. Everyone who has this hope purifies himself, just as He is pure." (NIV)

Salvation is the beginning of the Christian walk. This Christian walk begins with four principles, which are our biblical foundations for salvation and these are

Principle #1—God loves us and seeks to have a relationship with us.

John 3:16 states "For God so loved the world that He gave His only begotten Son, that whosoever believes in Him should not perish but have eternal life."
Definitions:
Eternal = without end
Believe = to accept as true, to trust, to have faith in
Perish = to become destroyed or ruined

Principle #2—Man is sinful and therefore separated from God.
Definition:
Sin = Thoughts or behavior which are contrary to the glory and character of God or to commit and offense against God's laws, statues, and commandments.

Man is sinful by choice, In that when God made man on the sixth day, He made him in His image, and God has a will. Therefore being in the image of God, man was also given a will. This gives man choices. Check for yourself the biblical basis found in scripture. Gen. 1:26-27, Gen. 2:15-18, the commandment was given to Adam, and woman was made as his helpmeet. Gen3: 1-6 Man's disobedience to the command of God brought sin into the world. Romans 3:10 "there is none righteous, no not one", Romans 3:23 "All have sinned and come short of the glory of God." Romans 6:23 "The wages of sin is death" (spiritual separation from God. This is what happened with Adam.

Principle #3—God's Provision

Definition:
Provision = to provide or make preparation for before hand

God's provision for man's sin is Jesus Christ alone.

Romans 5:8 "God demonstrates His own love toward us, in that while we were yet sinners Christ died for us" (KJV)

Christ died in our place, He shed his blood and according to 1 Corinthians 15:3-6 He was seen after His death and eyewitnesses are irrefutable evidence.

According to John 14:6 Jesus states that "I am the way, the truth, and the life, no one comes to the Father, but through Me."

Jesus bridged the gap between man and God.

Principle #4—Man's Decision

Man meaning you and I must make a decision to accept or reject this gift that has been prepared, and given for our salvation. We must receive this gift of God, which is Jesus Christ as Savior and Lord, in order to have a true relationship with God through His Son.

John 1:12 "as many as received Him, to them He gave the right become children of God even to those who believe on His name" (NKJV). We receive Christ through faith. Ephesians 2:8-9 states, "By grace you have been saved through faith; and that not of yourselves, it is the gift of God; not as a result of works that no one should boast" (NIV

This salvation involves commitment of our mind, emotions, and our will or volition.

When we speak of our mind this involves accepting and learning what scripture says about Him. Check out these scriptures: John1: 1-5, 12-14, Colossians 1:13-17, Colossians 2:9, Hebrews 1:1-3, and John 1:22-23.

Our emotions can be misleading and deceiving, We often look for chills or some sort of feeling that will prove that, once we have received Jesus as Savior and Lord, He indeed dwells within us, and this may actually happen to some, and to others it may not, as salvation is also progressive, to some there may be an instantaneous change, and with others it may take time for the changes that will take place in our lives to come.

As we grow spiritually, changes began to take place in four areas of our lives,

(1) Thoughts—our carnal thoughts become Godly thoughts (Rom. 12:12, Isa. 55:8-9,
(2) Desires—Instead of carnal, fleshly desires, our desires become Godly desires, Isa. 55:8-9 Ps.37: 4,
(3) Our words and things we say began to change to Godly words, Eph. 4:29-32, Eph. 5:4
(4) Our carnal activities become Godly or Christ centered activities. Gal.5: 15, 22-26.

Salvation Involves Our Will or Volition:

Our will or volition involves study of God's word and a commitment to apply it to our lives, for we alone have the choice to be obedient or disobedient to God's will for our lives, as John 14: 15 says "If you love Me, keep My commandments" (NKJV) and John 14: 21 states "He who has My commandments and keeps them, it is he who loves Me. And he who loves Me will be loved by My Father, and I will manifest Myself to him."

In applying God's word to our lives where we are, our goals also change from carnal, fleshly goals such as being all that we can be without God, to being more like Christ. This brings us to Romans 12:1-2. "I beseech you therefore, brethren by the mercies of God, that you present your bodies a living sacrifice, holy, acceptable unto God, which is your reasonable service. And be not conformed to this world, but be ye transformed by the renewing of your mind, that you may prove what is that good, and acceptable, and perfect will of God." (NIV). We can't do this unless we decide to obey God's word once we apply it to our lives, as Joshua 24: 15 states "choose you this day whom you will serve." The choice is yours, and not to choose is to choose.

The fist step in the transformation into His likeness involves a renewal of our self-concept based on the truth of the Scripture. Thereby, identifying the distorted way that we see ourselves, and consequently feel about ourselves. We find in 1 John 2: 12, that we are loved and forgiven unconditionally therefore we are secure in that love and significant as a son or daughter of God. Hence we can move from the sense of not being eligible for God's love and forgiveness, from self-condemnation, self-justification, and being motivated by reward and punishment, performing to please, pretense, and sabotaging our adult lives by being ashamed of who we are, understanding that and being confident that God accepts us in Christ, causing us to take off our mask and break the vase pretense and receive the healing that God wants us to have.

Now we can begin to live under grace and His non-repayable love, thereby experiencing divine healing of all of our hurts, bad habits, and cravings which tend to cripple us, and rely solely on God for everything. By forgiving us completely God obligates us to forgive ourselves and makes it a sin for us not to do so. What does this mean to you personally? Only you and answer this question.

We must understand that a heart set on worldly, carnal things lacks the power to resist sin. Such a mindset leads to death and eternal separation from God. (See Psalms 1:1-6 and Galatians 5:19-24).

Your personal relationship with the Father is to become increasingly rooted in both your assurance of salvation and you status as a son or daughter of God. Colossians 1:13-14 states "For He has rescued us from the dominion of darkness and brought us into the Kingdom of the Son He loves. In Whom we have redemption, the forgiveness of sins (fully forgiven), and your status as a son/daughter in Christ. And John 1: 12-12 says "Yet to all that received Him, to those who believe on His name, He gave the right to become the children of God (loved, secure and significant). For this reason we no longer have need to search for significance. 1 Peter 2: 9 states "But you are a chosen people, a royal priesthood, a holy nation belonging to God, that you may declare the praises of Him who called you out of the darkness into His marvelous light. Now we can live confident in our status as a child of God, loved unconditionally and fully assured of forgiveness of our sins, and living under the grace of God, which is that which we don't deserve.

This grace, which God gives, we can never repay, as it is not based on anything that we have done in our own volition or will, but on the blood of Jesus Christ our Lord and savior shed for our redemption on the cross at Calvary. In it we find liberty for where the Spirit is there is liberty. 2 Corinthians 3:17: "Now the Lord is the Spirit and where the Spirit of the Lord is there is liberty (freedom). (NIV)

We also find security in the Word of God. Specifically in 2 Corinthians 1: 20-22 which states "For all the promises of God in Him are yes, and in Him Amen, to the glory of God through us. Now He who establishes us with you in Christ and has anointed us is God, who also has sealed us and given us the Spirit in our hearts as a guarantee."

So many times we forget that we've been forgiven of all of our sins, past and present through the shed blood of Jesus Christ. And we begin to think and act as though our relationship with Him is based on just pleasing Him and others around us, and in doing this we make non-effect the true grace of God that has been given us by God through His Son Jesus. This means that we re-program our minds based on God's grace and unconditional love. For when we act as though our relationship with God is only based on our performance to please Him and those around us, we open ourselves up to the three battlegrounds that we have to contend with on a daily basis, and these are archenemies to the spiritual process of our growth in faith in God as a whole. These three battlegrounds are the world, the flesh, and the devil (Satan). When we open ourselves up to these battlegrounds we also open ourselves to thieves of God's grace. These are:

a) Thieves within ourselves: Among these are guilt, shame, self-condemnation, and self-justification (Hebrew 10:17 and Psalms 103:10-12)

b) Thieves within the Church: These include but are not limited to legalistic moralist, codified rules and regulations and conformity to "ought and should" (Colossians 1:6-8,20-23)

c) Thieves at home: Amongst these are thoughts and declarations of others in the family such as parents, who were to provide care, nurture, warmth and affection, but instead may have brought shame and disgrace by not treating us as the significant, trustworthy, and in the infinite worth that we were created to be. In turn making our own concept of our self to be flawed and cloud God's grace and wholeness, making our thought process and behavior reflect what has been said and done impacting our lives for the worse. (Ephesians 6:4 and Colossians 3:21)

d) Thieves within our culture: These are the areas in which we are categorized according to our culture, and rejected because of the difference that you may or may not have, or scorned by your own group, some may have looked on you as if you were an object rather than a person of worth. (Mark 4:19-20; Romans 12:2; 1 Corinthians 1:20)

e) Thieves in High Places: These are those influences in the spiritual realm of which Satan is the principle ruler. (Revelation 12:9-11)

Understand grace is what allows you to accept God's love and the truth that, in Christ you are worthy or that love. God's grace frees you from the need to please people, and thinking that you are inadequate or defective, while at the same time allowing you to live openly in His love, experiencing transparent friendships you have never known before, and receive His healing for your hurts and wounds that you have hidden in the closet of your temple.

With this grace you can break the vase of that rosebud that you wear daily allowing God to truly love and re-parent you as He desires to do, and experience His unconditional acceptance through Christ Jesus in your journey of faith.

Chapter 4

Forgiveness

V/S

Unforgiveness

Forgiveness v/s Unforgiveness

Forgiveness opens the door to the power of God, whereas unforgiveness robs us of that power, and the blessings of God in our lives.

Forgiveness plays a crucial part in the lives of the believer, as well as in society today. And yet it is one of the most misunderstood terms in today's society, mainly because forgiveness in not just a band aid for the surface of many of our hurts and wounds.

Why? Because many of these wounds are not just a surface scar that heals quickly, but they go so deep that they affect our emotional, spiritual and physical well being. When we don't forgive the whole man is affected.

This brings us to still another area just opposite of forgiveness is unforgiveness. Unforgiveness when not given proper and immediate attention, and is allowed to linger in our lives is detrimental, because it opens the door to spiritual bondage, as in the Spirit of Heaviness, the Spirit of Infirmity, the Spirit of Death, bitterness, and hardness of the heart.

How do we steer clear of these bondages? Well we forgive others their offenses as God forgave us. Eph. 4:29-32 tells us to let no corrupt word proceed out of your mouth, but what is good for necessary edification that it may impart grace to the hearers. And do not grieve the Holy Spirit of God, by whom you are sealed for the day of redemption. Let all bitterness, wrath, anger, clamor (which is loud boisterous complaining), and evil speaking be put away from you with all malice, and be kind to one another, tenderhearted, forgiving one another, as God in Christ forgave you.

You must deal with your heart, forgive, forget, let it go, that your prayers are not hindered. When we don't forgive, we put a nuce around our neck that invites Satan to freely work through causing our prayers to be empty, idle, unproductive, and all of your words of faith just hit the ceiling and bounce off, because we ourselves allowed Satan to place a snare around our necks through bitterness and strife. Mark 11:25-26 says: "And when you stand praying if you have anything against anyone forgive him, that your Father in heaven may also forgive you your trespasses. But if you do not forgive, neither will your Father in heaven forgive you your trespasses."

This kind of forgiveness reserves fellowship amongst believers. Our forgiveness must be beyond measure as in Matthew 18:21-35, where Jesus speaks of continual forgiveness, and in Luke 17:1-4 where Jesus teaches forgiveness. We must understand that there is no measure to forgiveness.

Unforgiveness is like a cancer; it kills and destroys from within by inward invasion. Unforgiveness and strife run deep, and a band-aid of prayer will not cure it. Unforgiveness and strife run hand in hand.

So you ask what then is strife. Strife is a bitter conflict or dissension between two or more persons.

24

Just as we must forgive, there are times that we ourselves need to be forgiven for our own actions. Sometimes we wound, in the way we treat people, often times we are judgmental, we gossip, we make differences, and sometimes we are just down right mean to one another, often taking advantage of our sisters and brothers in Christ. Often we get caught up in our own self-righteousness, and our own cares that we fail to feel the needs of or have compassion for those around us, we often forget that God along sets the standards for our lives.

This means that we must not open the door for confusion and evil through discord and strife. We must avoid strife at all cost. For strife is a luxury we cannot afford. That something about our brother or sister's personality that may affect us wrongly, or ticks us off, just may be relevant of a weakness in our own personality that needs to be dwelt with. Through fervent prayer, if we give that thing over to God, we may ourselves be changed or delivered from that personality flaw.

Actual Causes of Strife

1. Doctrinal Disputes—1 Timothy 6:3-4
2. Carnal Mindedness—1 Corinthians 3: 1-9
3. Contentions Men & Women—Proverbs 26:17-21
4. Disputes between Men & Women—Gen 13: 1-7
5. Self Ambition & Pride—Luke 22: 24-27

Unforgiveness can break up an ordained team by one or a number of persons sowing discord amongst the brethren, through the means of gossip and lies. Proverb 6:16-19

Unforgiveness hinders prayers between husbands and wives.
1 Peter 3:7-8.

Unforgiveness hinders us from receiving revelation knowledge because of the hardness of our heart and the carnality of the mind. 1 Corinthians 3:1-3.

Unforgiveness hinders the manifestation of the Gifts of the Spirit.
1 Corinthians 13: 1-3

Pride Causes Contention—Proverb 13:10

Forgiveness is somewhat like baking a cake. Just as there are ingredients in the preparation of a cake, so are there ingredients for preparing the heart for forgiveness.

Five Steps in Preparing the Heart for Forgiveness

1. Put off the old man or nature—Ephesians 4:24-32
2. Confess our sins of unforgiveness and strife—1 John 1:9
3. Receive your forgiveness/forgive yourself
4. Forget it, let it go, and refuse to bring it up again.
5. Praise God for your freedom from the bondage of unforgiveness

Forgiveness is your path to freedom reflecting God's action, our reaction, and God's word.

To have open hands and forgiving hearts we must learn and know the affects of unforgiveness and strife on our lives, for it indeed affects the whole man. 2 Timothy 2:14-22 states (If, meaning a condition must be met) if we purge ourselves from strife and unforgiveness, we shall be vessels unto honor, sanctified and meet for the masters use, and prepared unto every good work.

The Bible says that the Word of God is as a two edged sword. The sword being the Word of God itself, the first edge to be used in Spiritual Warfare against the enemy (Satan), and the second edge is to be used as a purging instrument for cleansing us from sin.

With this in mind let us prepare our hearts for freedom with this prayer.

Heavenly Father,

In the name of Jesus, I forgive each and every one and anyone, who has offended me, no matter what was said or done. I forgive them in the name of Jesus. And if I have offended anyone, I ask you to forgive me for that, and reveal them to me, that I may control them. I will put off the old nature and put on my new nature, and in Jesus name I now receive my forgiveness and my cleansing. I am now free from strife and dissension, form envy, from jealousy, because I purge myself with the Word of God and command these enemies to my stability to get out and stay out of my life. I refuse to regard iniquity in my mind and heart, and therefore my prayers will not be hindered. So Father, I now confess before you the sin of unforgiveness, and now receive my forgiveness. I am committed to forget it, I will let it go, and I will never bring it up again, it is over. I will allow you to heal my hurts and my wounds, and I praise you for my freedom form the bondage of unforgiveness.

Amen.

Chapter 5

Making

Christ

King

Making Christ King

Your new nature will produce fruit. It is often said that you can tell a tree by the fruit it bares. The fruit of the Spirit is not what you do, but what you are. The fruit of each of the two natures, both old and new describes character not your activities.

Since the time you chose to receive Christ as Lord and savior of your life, He began to sit on the throne of your heart, and the quality of your character assures that Christ permanently dwells within you.

As every tree bears fruit, there is absolute no excuse for not producing fruit. Your relationship with Christ through prayer helps you to be sensitive to the Holy Spirit. Prayer is having conversation with Christ. The word of God tells us to be anxious for nothing but in every thing through prayer and supplication, let your request be known unto God. Not knowing what to say to Christ is no excuse for not praying. Christ can express your interest and innermost thoughts in silent prayer if you allow Him. The Holy Spirit prays for us in "groans that words cannot express" Romans 8:26. You do not have to struggle to be like Jesus. You simply choose to allow Him to be himself within you. Remember that the old nature stills wants to control you. You make the choice moment by moment.

Because Christ changes our attitudes and actions on day-by-day bases, we cannot use the excuse that unchristian behavior and attitudes cannot be said to just be our human nature. Read Romans 6:12-18, to fully understand fully about your old nature. To choose to allow our old nature to take control is to allow sin in our life.

Recognizing that Christ lives in you, all of his characteristics fully indwell you, because His life is the very essence of these qualities. The source of all your gifts and abilities are in Him alone. Colossians 3:1-7 gives us the rules or commands for living holy, and our daily walk with the Lord.

It is often stated that we must be baptized, and this is inline with the Great Commission that has been given to the church found in Matthew 28:19-20.

Even though this commission was originally given to the disciples, it still holds true for today. The baptism is symbolic of the death, burial, and resurrection of Jesus Christ. In your life and mine it symbolizes the death and burial of the old nature and the resurrection of the new nature, which is in the indwelling Christ. Your salvation is in Jesus Christ alone.

As we yield ourselves and allow Christ to take full control of our lives, He becomes the controller of our new nature. The whole choice is one of obedience to the word of God and His commands. Reading the word of God and prayer is not enough; you must also be a doer of the Word. In other words you must apply the word of God to your life daily, and make the commitment to obey each command that the Lord gives and to have quiet times with Him that you may know His voice when He speaks to you.

Your new nature does not automatically remove everything that may lead you astray from the old nature, just because you have given your life to Christ. The old nature cannot be changed and is not to be trusted. Your old nature is not dead. They both struggle to gain control, but you make the decision to allow the Holy Spirit to take full charge.

Chapter 6

Service

Service

"The Son of Man came not into the world to be served, but to serve, and to give His life as a ransom for many . . ." Matthew 20:28

A working definition of service is to respond to the needs of others in specific areas in a functioning capacity.

Biblically speaking service then is using ones gifts to serve others, glorify God, edify people, and to further the Kingdom of God.

We must understand that reasonable service does end at the sacrifice of our bodies to God. Being that our bodies have now become the temple of God after salvation, it includes the study and application of Gods' word to our lives. This also means a change in lifestyle, allowing a relationship with the Father, and Him manifesting Himself in every area of our lives through the Fruit of The Spirit. (Gal. 5:22-23) "But the fruit of the Spirit is love, joy, peace, long-suffering (patience), gentleness, goodness, faith, meekness, temperance (self-control), against such there is no law." (NIV).

Traditionally, ways of serving in the church were Choir, Usher Board, Deacon Board, Sunday School Teacher, and volunteers in the kitchen, and still are in some of the smaller churches. (*Smaller only denotes to membership size*). One would serve where assigned and not according to their spiritual gifting, passion of purpose, and thus not be fulfilled in their service. Today there are mega-churches (*Large Memberships)* and many ministries which cover many areas of ministry and one is more likely to serve according to passion purpose and gifting if these are known and according to the knowledge of spiritual gifts and beliefs of the visionary or Shepherd of the house or local church. This can also be done in the smaller churches as well.

So we come to the question, why should we serve? For one there is no ministry called pew in the local church. It is not enough to just attend church on Saturday, Sunday or whatever day of the week that has been set aside for worship. And get fat and spiritually constipated on the scrumptious spiritual meals that are prepared and served by the men and women or God, but to be balanced by exercising and sharing what we have (eaten) just taken in, by glorifying God, and edifying people, according to 1 Peter 4:11, 1 Corinthians 12:7, and Ephesians 4:12. And we glorify God and edify people to fulfill the Great Commandment, which says, "Love the Lord your God with all your heart, soul, and all your might, and love your neighbor as yourself. Matthew 22:37-39.

This in itself tells us that we must serve in love as we discover and use our gifts as well as our talents. As we serve we find that we meet the needs of people in three areas. Physical (Matt. 25:35-36, 40) Emotional (1 Thess. 5:14) and Spiritual (2 Corinthians 5:18; Col. 1:28-29)

> ***Understand that service is work in every since of the word and to be a servant of God is to be a servant of the people***

Where and how you will serve in the Body of Christ will be determined by your availability or the time you can set aside for service in ministry. Your spiritual maturity, which covers the level of your maturity spiritually, as there may be some areas of ministry you, would not place a novice or babe in Christ. And your flexibility, which covers your personality, and how much time you have for ministry, and timing as well, as you must remain balanced. There must also be time for family, work, friends, study and other important areas of your life.

We often look for people to mentor us in ministry, if you cannot find one that you feel meets the qualifications of a true mentor, look to Jesus Christ, because the ultimate servant is Jesus Christ. (Matt. 20:28)

When we really look at the attributes of a servant we look for one who ultimately has these qualities:

1. **A Servant is Unselfish**
2. **A Servant is a Giver**
3. **A Servant is a Forgiver**
4. **A Servant is a Forgetter**

5. **A Servant is Influential**
6. **A servant is Obedient**
7. **A Servant is Humble**
8. **A Servant is a Peacemaker**

*Understand that these qualities come as a process of Spiritual Growth and Spiritual Growth does not come automatically. *

When we look at a servant, who has possessed, and allowed God to conquer his/her heart. We see the imaginary of a canvas, where in is a portrait of the biblical beatitudes found in Matthew 5:7-12.

Blessed are the merciful, for they shall receive mercy.
Blessed are the pure in heart, for they shall see God.
Blessed are the peacemakers, for they shall be called the sons of God.
Blessed are those who are persecuted for righteousness sake, for theirs is the Kingdom of Heaven.
Blessed are you when men revile you, and persecute you and say all kinds of evil against you falsely, for My sake.
Rejoice and be exceeding glad, for great is your reward in heaven for so they persecuted the prophets who were before you.

As we look at each of these beatitudes, each one is followed by a promise from the Father. To be a truly authentic servant of God, we must with God's help give of ourselves, with a passion for serving wherever, and wherever without recognition, reservation, reluctance or restriction. This is truly a rare find in today's society.

In order to do this we must come to understand the biblical perspective of servant hood, through self-evaluation and application of the Word of God in our individual lives. We must then truly come to the reality as God's word says; "Being confident of this very thing, that He who begun a good work in you will complete it until the day of Jesus Christ." (Phil.1: 6). In this knowing that it is not we doing the work but the Father, in and through us.

Chapter 7
Passion
As   It
Relates
to
Purpose

Passion as it Relates to Purpose

First let's look at what passion is in the first place, in other words what is passion.

Passion is a strong desire or interest in a certain people, cause, or role in which one desires to make a difference.

Funk & Wagnall defines passion as an intense or overpowering emotion, or an eager outreaching of mind toward some specific object, or strong impulse tending to physical indulgence.

Bruce Bugbee in his book "What You Do Best In The Body of Christ" (Zondervan Publishing House 1974) Defines passion as "The God-given desire that compels us to make a difference in a particular area of ministry in life where God is glorified and people are edified."

So then with this in mind, passion reveals the hearts' desire. So how do we relate this desire/passion in the spiritual sense of the word? Psalms 37:3-4 says, "Trust in the Lord and do good. Dwell in the land and feed on His faithfulness. Delight yourself also in the Lord and He shall give you the desires of your heart." We often take this text to only mean the materialist desires that we have, especially those of us that are new to the faith, and some of us that are not so new to the faith.

Although material desires can be included in these desires, we must understand that after salvation, and trusting in the Lord, He gives us His desires for us, which become our desires out of our desire to be all that He wants us to be, as we allowing Him to be Lord of our lives and to sit on the throne of our hearts and take total control.

When on the other hand scripture tell us "But seek ye first the Kingdom of God and His righteousness, and all these things will be added to you" Matt. 6:33 (KJV). The all these things are the material things that will automatically come with the seeking of the Kingdom and His righteousness in God's timing.

How then do we know that our desire is our God given passion? Well in seeking to find out if our desire/passion is our God-given desire/passion, just as we test things in the secular sense we must also test them in the spiritual sense to see if they are of God.

Bruce Bugbee in his book *What You Do Best in the Body of Christ*, (Zondervan Publishing House 1974) states that "the testing of our passion is two fold. It should answer two questions. (1) Does it glorify God? (2) Does it edify others?" I would like to add a third question to that test. (3) Does it further the Kingdom of God? If it does not meet this test, then you have not yet identified your God-given passion. This passion will reveal where you desire to serve in the Body of Christ.

There are several hindrances to identifying your passion, such as past rejection, low self esteem, or fear to name a few. But we must understand that years of disappointment, rejection and suppression will not change your passion. Because it is God-given, and given to be expressed. Now that we know what passion is and that it comes from God.

Uncovering your passion is not always easy; as well as; fulfilling your passion is not always fun. As you become more discipline in your prayer life and service, the revelation of your passion will come.

This is just the beginning of your journey towards fulfilling your purpose, passion, and using your gifts. Serving in ministry along with prayer will cause your passion to become evident. This vision or dream is unique and only you can complete or fulfill it. This dream may also be fulfilled beyond the walls of the Sanctuary. Now understand that this will require obedience to the vision or dream that God has given to you along with His statues, commandments, and laws.

Now once I find my God given passion or desire, where then do I serve within the Body of Christ? Well this will depend on the desire or passion. If you have a passion for children, you should then serve in a ministry committed to impacting the lives of children. On the other hand if your desire or passion is for world hunger, you should serve in a ministry or organization committed to feeding the poor.

Proverbs 19: 21 say, "Many are the plans of a man's heart, but the Lord's purpose, that will prevail." (NIV) "The human mind may devise many plans, but it is the purpose of the Lord's that will be established." (NRSV)

This brings us to the question, what is purpose?

Purpose is:

   a) The original intent for a creation.
   b) The original reason for the existence of a thing.
   c) The end for which the means exist
   d) The destination that prompts the journey
   e) The expectation of the source a product

Having a working idea of what purpose is, we can now understand that God has a plan and a purpose for our lives, not just from the time of salvation, but from the very moment of conception. Jeremiah 29: 11 states "For I know the plans that I have for you, says the Lord, plans of good and not of evil, to give you a future and a hope." (NIV) And "Being confident of this very thing that He who begun a good work in you will complete it until the day of Christ Jesus" Phil. 1:6. (NIV)

With a working definition of a purpose or calling, you are probably asking yourself, where do I fit into this equation, or what about me? Well the answer is yes you too have been called for a purpose and been given at least one spiritual gift. Now you must understand, you are now accountable for that which you know. According to 1 Peter 4:10 each of us has received a gift according to the manifold grace of God. According to 1Timothy 4: 14a, it is a sin to hide or neglect the use of your gift or gifts.

We are equipped and empowered with gifts by God in order to fulfill or complete our purpose or call. So we come to yet another question. What is a Spiritual Gift? Well a Spiritual Gift is a special attribute given by the Holy Spirit to every member of the Body of Christ, according to God's grace, for use within the context of the Body of Christ, to complete the individual purpose of each member of the Body of Christ functioning together in community, complementing each other in the local congregations as well as outside the walls of the local church. Which at the same time is evidenced in his/her ministry, for the edification and maturing of the Body of Christ and the furtherance of the Kingdom of God.

Now that we know what a Spiritual Gift is we must also understand what a Spiritual Gift is not. Spiritual Gifts are not Psychics, occult, natural talents, cooking, dancing, singing, counterfeit gifts (those given by Satan or use for the glorification of his kingdom) Christian roles, Evangelism or your choice. In order to fulfill God's plan and purpose for your life you must operate in your spiritual gifts.

Understand that the more you pray, and the more you serve in those areas that are fulfilling, the more your God given passion and purpose will be revealed.

Chapter 8

Stewardship

Stewardship

**"As each one has received a gift, minister
it to one another, as good stewards of the
manifold grace of God." (NIV)**

In the simplest terms, stewardship is when one is or has been entrusted with that which belongs to another. In the context of our lessons we speak of that which God has entrusted in each of us as part of the Body of Christ, whether spiritual blessings, material or financial blessings.

According to scripture we as Christians are stewards of our spiritual gifts. 1 Peter 4: 10 states, "As each one has received a gift, minister it to one another, as good stewards of the manifold grace of God." So Christians are intern accountable to God for the discovery of and the use of their individual spiritual gifts, which are spiritually discerned.

Every spiritual gift is given as a resource that we must use and will be held accountable at the judgment. Some will have one, some two, some five or more. Each of us is given at least one spiritual gift. We are the stewards of these gifts and are responsible only for what the Holy Spirit has chosen to give to us. These must be used to complete or accomplish the purpose or call that has been given each of us. For that purpose or call is a unique and different as one's DNA or fingerprints.

Ignorance of these gifts will not hold up for each is listed in scripture in the following passages: 1 Corinthians 2, 1 Corinthians 12, Romans 12, and Ephesians 4. In our studies you will become aware of these and the list of the gifts. Then understand that once you know what they are and the ones that have been bestowed upon you by the Holy Spirit you are accountable for their use and not to abuse them.

Stewardship also involves commitment to the will of God, and the call and purpose that God has ordained for your life specifically. Not to swell your head but you must understand that you have been uniquely made in the image of God Himself, skillfully and wonderfully made and when God made and molded you and is still molding you into the person He says that you are. He broke the mold; there is no one like you. And the call, the plan, and the purpose that God has for your life is just that unique. For he has ordered your steps, just as it was ordained that you would be reading this book, right now. His purpose for you, only you can do. And when you fell to do so, then the work of ministry is incomplete.

All the tools you need have already been given you. It is all about timing, His timing and not yours. It all calls for consecration, worship, praise, intercession, preparation, revelation, conformation and manifestation of the work of ministry that God has assigned and called you to in love.

Those who refuse to discover God's plan, and operate in their spiritual gifts on the grounds that they would somehow become arrogant and prideful, fail to understand the biblical teachings about the gifts of the spirits, or their motive are wrong, and they don't want the accountability that their gifts and God's purpose for their life will bring for its use, either way they are being disobedient to the word of God concerning spiritual gifts.

Seven Principles of Good Stewardship

1. Everything we own actually belongs to God (Psalms 24: 1)
2. Giving produces Joy (Luke 6: 38)
3. Give by faith (Philippians 4: 19)
4. What you sow you will reap (2 Corinthians 9: 10)
    a) Give to honor God (1 Timothy 5:8)
    b) Give from the heart (2 Corinthians 5: 9)
    c) God wants you to be prosperous. (Philippians 4: 19)

To be a good steward of the plan that God has for your life. You must respond, and there are only two responses that you can make.

If your response is yes then you will be serving in ministry and walking in that plan or purpose.

If your response is no then you will find yourself stagnated, and feeling that you are not growing spiritually, or you are at this time settled into a comfort zone of complacency. Take some time out and read about Moses plight when God gave him instructions about his purpose. (Exodus chapters 3 and 4) Do you see yourself in any of these areas? Well if not, then what hinders you from saying yes to the plan and purpose that God has for your life?

Or may be you might find yourself amongst these four foundational barriers. The I syndrome of pride, Anxious with fear (false evidence appearing real), what's in it for me syndrome of selfishness, and the I can't syndrome of unbelief.

Chapter 9

Suffering

Suffering

**"But rejoice that you participate in the sufferings
of Christ, so that you may be overjoyed
when His glory is revealed." 1 Peter 4:13**

Let us now discuss the fact of suffering. Understand we are not only called to salvation, but we are also called to suffer. Just as our memory verse above says, that we are to rejoice when we suffer. The Holy Spirit will teach us how to suffer, and overcome our trials and persecutions, remembering that if you don't have a head on collision with the enemy, or Satan, you are traveling in the same direction as he, and carnality, sin and salvation do not travel parallel. And will in the end reach different eternal places, either heaven or hell. These are real places. They are not fictitious, nor are they a part of a fairy tale.

You must choose your travel or journey. And to not choose is to choose. The world hated Jesus and thus will also hate you if you name the name of Jesus. If you have accepted Jesus as Savior and Lord of your life, you are a new creature in Christ Jesus, but Satan has assigned one of his demons to torment you and cause you to return to the sinful lifestyle. So understand that you are in a good place when you suffer for righteousness. This means that you are doing damage to the kingdom of Satan. Remember the scripture says "Greater is He that is in you than he that is in the world." 1 John 4:4.

To get a working definition for suffer; this word comes from the Greek word Pascho. Webster's Dictionary defines it as: to undergo or feel pain, to sustain damage or loss. In other words to suffer is to endure violence, ill treatment, roughness or evils from without.

Philippians 1: 27-29 expressly tells us to let our conduct be worthy of the gospel of Christ, whatever our circumstances, and to not terrified of our adversaries, for we have been granted on behalf of Christ, not only to believe in Him but also to suffer for His sake.

Remember that no weapon that is formed against you shall prosper. This is not to say that weapons will not be formed, but when we take up our shield of faith in Jesus, every fiery dart will be canceled.

Acts 1:9 lets us know that the Father will show us, just as He did Paul, how many things we must suffer for His name sake. So don't quit, continue to do damage to Satan's territory.

Many of you have gone through hell and high water, to reach this point in your lives, but understand that it is for ministry, that you have suffered. Nothing just happens. For God to use you mightily, He must break you (that breaking is sometimes painful) that you might minister and serve others by relating to their hurts effectively.

The question comes to mind, "If you have not walked in my shoes, how can you relate to my problems or sufferings, or what I am going through." The anointing that God places on your life as well as the gifts are without repentance and you must be able to withstand the weight of this anointing, which will lead to your actual call or purpose. God will not put more on you than you can handle, and He knows how much you can take. So if you are in a season of suffering, or trials, understand that you can handle it. Because God has already placed what it takes to handle everything that you will ever go through, in you.

Chapter 10

Moving Into The Next

Era of Divine Purpose

Moving to the Next Era of Divine Purpose

For every trip or journey that we take there must be preparation and in this book you have allowed me to help you in that preparation for moving to the next stage, level or era of your divine purpose.

God's word says that for everything there is a season and a time for every purpose under heaven. So what then is the ultimate plan or purpose for man? I am glad you asked, the ultimate purpose for man is to glorify God relationally both vertically and horizontally according to scripture.

We have been given a mandate or commandment. And the commandment that we were given is that we love one another (John13: 34-35) "A new commandment I give you. That you love one another; as I have loved you, that you also love one another. By this all will know that you are my disciples, if you love one another." This tells us that in every thing that we do to glorify God, edify His people, and further His kingdom we must do it in love. Otherwise it is of null effect, which takes us to the reference of 1 Corinthians chapter 13, which tells us that although we have these gifts, and realize the plan that God has for our lives, when we operate in them without love we become like sounding brass and tingling cymbals. There is no profit in the use of our gifts in the Body of Christ without love.

So let's look at some of the scriptures we have used previously.

1 Peter 4:10: "Each one should use whatever gift he has received to serve others, faithful administrating God's grace in its various forms.

Each gift was given to complete the purpose or assignment or call that has been set for us to do in our lifetime here on earth, to glorify Him, edify His people, and further His kingdom in love.

What does it mean to glorify God, edify His people, and to further His kingdom? Well to glorify means to exalt or to magnify, or give honor. To edify means to build up in the faith. And to further the kingdom of God is to do everything you can to advance His kingdom.

Now in order to build one another up in the faith, give honor, exalt, please God and advance His kingdom. We must have a relationship with Him, which also requires a dialogue, as there is no relationship without dialogue. This means that we must communicate with God the father. And we do this by means of prayer. So you ask; what actually is prayer?

Prayer is the sincere desire of the heart, in other words holding a conversation with God. To do this we must know His word, so we can pray according to His will, and not amiss. This also requires true salvation, which is the first step toward true Christianity. Accepting Christ Jesus as Savior and allowing Him to be Lord of you life, relinquishing your will, or volition to Him, and spending time with Him, as you would a girl or boy friend.

Also required is to choose to be obedient to His word, laws, statues and commands. This takes us to the reference in Deuteronomy 28: 1-14 which cover the blessings of obedience.

Deuteronomy 28: 15-68 covers the curses of disobedience. Check them out, and remember the choice is yours. These are still relative in today's society.

Christ understands that the temptations and the trials that we each encounter. Hebrew 4: 14 tells us how this is done. Jesus is touched by our weakness and temptations but yet He is without sin. Why? Because He was tempted just as we are. Jesus lived this life and made Himself a perfect example of how to live this life without fear of falling into the bondage of temptations and sin itself. Meditate on 1 Corinthians 10:13, and consider your belief in the understanding that Jesus was tempted just as we ourselves are today and that He understands and is willing and able to help us in every situation we may face.

Because of the struggles we go through on a daily basis, we ask ourselves several questions. Will we ever be rid of the old or sin nature? Will the time ever come when our new nature does not have a daily struggle with the old nature? Well the answer is yes. When Christ returns, we will be totally set free of the presence and influence of the old sin nature.

In consideration of 1 Peter 1:6-9, this passage of scripture refers to the triangle of salvation, past, present and future. It refers to your faith in Jesus Christ, whom you have never seen with your physical eyes, the trials you are going through now, which prove the genuineness of your faith, and testing of your faith with fire, which will result in praise, glory, and honor. At the revealing of Jesus Christ at His second coming, you will receive your promised inheritance, which is eternal life.

Jeremiah 29:11: "For I know the thoughts that I think toward you, says the Lord, thoughts of peace and not evil to give you a future and a hope." (NKJV)

This lets us know that God had a plan for each or our lives, before we were even conceived. 1 Peter 2; 9 tells us that "you are a chosen generation, a royal priesthood, a holy nation, His own special people, that you may proclaim the praises of Him who called you out of darkness into His marvelous light.

You must also know that there are foundational barriers that hinder us from saying yes to the call and plans that God has for our lives, which are:

1. Pride: The "I, me and my" syndrome
2. Fear: The "I can't" syndrome (False evidence appearing real)
3. Selfishness: The "What's in it for me" syndrome
4. Unbelief: The "I am not qualified or good enough" syndrome.

Philippians 1:6: "Being confident of this very thing He which hath begun a good work in you will perform it until the day of Jesus Christ." (NIV)

This is the same confidence that you had when you sat in that chair. You didn't check to see if it would hold you, or if it was sturdy enough to hold your weight. You must know that you know, that you know that the passion and vision that God has given to you, regardless of the circumstances, He will provide for and complete the call using the gifts He has already placed in you and that you have spiritually discerned.

Proverbs 16:9 states that "a man's heart plans his way. But the Lord directs his steps."

Proverb 37:23 states that "the steps of a good man are ordered by the Lord."

Being confident means trust, regardless of the situation that we find ourselves in. And because we are confident that God will bring to completion that which He, Himself has begun in us, we can be content in the state we find ourselves, knowing that no weapon that is formed against us will prosper, not that the weapons won't be formed, but because God has already established the end, He alone is omniscient, omnipresent, and omnipotent. He protects us from the destruction of any weapon formed.

God demonstrated His love for us in that, while we were yet sinners, Christ died for us. This brings us to another scripture reference.

Matthew 20:28: "the Son of Man did not come to be served, but to serve and give His life as a ransom for many." (NKJV)

Just as Christ was a good steward over what God the Father, entrusted in Him, knowing what His purpose was and choosing to say yes to the Father, He humbled Himself and became obedient to the point of death, even the death of the cross. There are rewards for being good stewards over the gifts and the callings, which God has assigned to your very lives. Proof being that God highly exalted Jesus Christ and gave Him the name, which is above every name. That at the name of Jesus every knee should bow, of those in heaven, and those on earth, and those under the earth, and that every tongue should confess that Jesus Christ is Lord, to the glory of God the Father.

Acts 1:8: "But ye shall receive power, after that the Holy Ghost is come upon you; and ye shall be witnesses unto Me both in Jerusalem, and in all Judea, and in Samaria, and unto the uttermost part of the earth." (NIV)

Because we now have that same power of the Holy Ghost (Holy Spirit) within us, as well as upon us, greater is He that is in us than He that is in the world. Now with that same power, in as much as we are accountable for what we know, we must fulfill the Great Commission of Jesus Christ, which is:

Matthew 28:18-20: "And Jesus came and spake unto them, saying, all power is given unto Me in heaven and in earth. Go ye therefore and teach all nations, baptizing them in the name of the Father, and of the Son, and of the Holy Ghost: Teaching them to observe all things whatsoever I have commanded you: and lo, I am with you even unto the end of the world. Amen." (NIV)

Chapter 11

Pick Up Your Shield

And Trust The Captain

Pick Up Your Shield and Trust the Captain

**Trust in the Lord with all thine heart, and lean
not to your own understanding. In all thy ways
acknowledge Him and He will direct thy paths.
Proverbs: 3:5-6**

Definitions:

Shield: A defensive peace of armor
Faith: Confidence in the testimony of another, without proof
Trust: To put ones' confidence in another
Captain: A title expressing leadership

How often do we think we can make it on our own merits, or that the task set before us in impossible, only to find our after struggling with it, we couldn't accomplish it on our own. We worry about it, we fret over it, and we are so busy doing our own thing that we forget to pray. We want our walk with the Lord to be a successful one, but when that doesn't happen, we are ready to just give up and quit the race.

Philippians 4:13 say "I can do all things through Christ who strengthens me."

In order to believe this we must first believe that Christ is and has the power to work within us.

Often times we have more faith in the chairs we set in daily, believing that the chair will hold us up. We just sit down without even think about it.

In this life we must remember that our warfare is not physical but spiritual. The Bible says "But without faith it is impossible to please Him, for he that cometh to God must believe that He is, and He is a rewarder of them that diligently seek Him. Hebrews 11:6.

In order to seek Him we must pray. Prayer is our means of communication with God.

Matthew 7:7-8 says, "ask and it shall be given you, seek and ye shall find, knock and it shall be opened. For everyone that ask receiveth, and he that seeketh findeth and to him that knocketh it shall be opened.

Now that we know what the word of God says about asking, seeking, and knocking, we must also realize that we must exercise the faith that God has already given to us, to reach our in the authority that is ours in Christ Jesus, through the power of the Holly Spirit filling and flowing through us, the sick will be healed, the demon possessed delivered, and the lost will be saved.

This same faith, through Gods' word and His promises is also a great part of the armor that God has given us for the spiritual warfare that we fight daily. The Bible calls it our shield in Ephesians 6:16, which states and I quote: "Above all, taking on the shield of faith, where ye shall be able to quench the fiery darts of the wicked."

Nelsons' Concordance defines shield as a defensive piece of armor. This shield coupled with trust in our captain, which is our Lord and savior Jesus Christ, who continues to direct our paths regardless of the circumstances and pitfalls, that lye before us, believing without a doubt that through this shield of faith the Lord will protect and keep us. It is not enough to just have faith; we must act upon that faith. The Bible says faith without works is dead.

There is and old song called, The Old Ship of Zion. In this song the writer states: tis the old Ship of Zion, 'Tis The Old Ship of Zion, 'Tis The Old Ship of Zion, get on board, get on board. The writer goes on to say, "It has landed many a thousand, get on board. The writer ends the song by telling us who the captain is. "King Jesus is the Captain, get on board, get on board.

Now since we know that Jesus is the captain, the head of our lives, and the author and finisher of our faith. Lets not jump ship, for the working of our faith has just begun. Jesus has brought us through so many dangers seen and unseen, toils and snares, and some we didn't know we were in. We must have that same faith we had in the chair we sit in, in Jesus, knowing that He will do what He said and promised, and abundantly more that we could even ask or think. Our circumstances are just opportunities for the Holy Spirit to work in and through us. And I truly want to hear Him say well done. Don't you?

Thoughts to Remember
I Take the shield of faith to quench the fiery darts of the wicked
II Trust the captain not our own understanding
III Acknowledge Him always for directions

Chapter 12

Spiritual Armor

&

Weapons of Warfare

Spiritual Armor and Weapons of Warfare

"Finally, my brethren, be strong in the Lord, and in the power of His might. Put on the whole armor of God that ye may be able to stand against the wiles of the devil. For we wrestle not against flesh and blood, but against powers, against the rulers of darkness of this world, against spiritual wickedness in high Places. Wherefore take unto you the whole armor of God that you may be able to withstand in the evil day, and having done all, to stand. Stand therefore, having your loins girt about with truth, and having on the breastplate of righteousness; and your feet shod with the preparation of the gospel of peace; above all, taking one the shield of faith, wherewith ye shall be able to quench all the fiery darts of the wicked. And take on the helmet of salvation, and the sword of the Spirit, which is the word of God: Praying always with all prayer and supplication in the Spirit, and watching thereunto with all preservation and supplication for all saints." Ephesians 6:10-18 (NIV)

Please understand that God has not left us with out any weapons to fight with, He also gave us armor to wear, even when we are not at war. This war we call Spiritual Warfare.

Let's go through each of them carefully with an explanation.

Verses 10-12 establish the fact that we are in a war. This war is Spiritual. When you accepted Jesus Christ as your personal savior and allowed Him to become Lord of your life, if you were really serious about this decision, you also joined the army of the kingdom of God. Verses 13-18, tells us what kind of clothing or armor as the word states we must wear in order to fight in this war.

Our loins must be girt with truth, your loin is your waist or abdomen, we wear a belt around our waist, and this belt must be filled with the truth of Gods word. We must continuously wear the breastplate of righteousness; the breastplate protects your chest and those delicate organs, such as your heart, lungs, and kidneys. The righteousness comes from application of Gods word in our lives, in other words, living the word, for we are the righteousness of God in Jesus Christ.

Our feet must be shod with the preparation of the gospel of peace. To be shod means to be covered, our feet must be protected, and through every journey that we travel there must be preparation for that journey, and we need the peace of God as we travel, and the gospel brings peace in every area, the valleys and the mountains.

The Shield of faith: Each of us is given a measure of faith, and it is impossible to please God without faith. This shield is for our protection. Every soldier caries a shield. But must discern where the weapons of the enemy are coming from, the word of God says that we shall be able to quench all of the fiery darts of the wicked. The wicked are our enemies. But no weapon that is formed against us will prosper; because God encamps His angels round about us for our protection. The weapons will be formed but they will not be successful.

The helmet was the first piece of armor you were given at the moment of salvation. The helmet covers your head, your mind, and your mental heart, your nose for smell, your mouth for proclamation of the word of God, to proclaim the word of God you must at all times have the sword of the Spirit. You must carry it in your mental heart that you may not sin against God. This means we must study and apply God's word to our lives right were we are in our spiritual growth. This is a matter of the heart.

Our weapons of defense are prayer, praise and worship. The word of God says that we are to pray always with all prayers and supplication in the Spirit. This means both in your understanding, and in your Spiritual Language (also known as tongues). Prayer is having a dialogue with and communicating the sincere desire of the heart to God in the name of Jesus Christ His Son.

Praise on the other hand is honoring Him, for what He is in your life, telling Him that you love Him and why, declaring His majesty, His faithfulness, His glory, Thanking Him for what He has done, is doing and is about to do in your life. What does He mean to you? This means the lifting of the hands, the shedding of tears, the dance, singing in the Spirit as at this point you may begin to praise Him in your spiritual language or tongues, these tongues need no interpretation as it is for your edification not the body of Christ as you speak mysteries by the leading of the Holy Spirit, who intercedes for us in groans that cannot be uttered in our natural language. Praise leads us into worship.

Please understand that everyone can praise and pray, but everyone cannot worship God. For worshiping God requires no exercise of the body, for you have then traveled into the Holies of Holies, which is in the presence of the most high God. When you reach it, stay there, and don't be in a hurry, enjoy the tranquility, the peace, and the true love of God. You are in the presence of the most high, the almighty God in Heaven. Allow Him to speak to you and hold you in the hollow of His hands, feel His grace and His mercy, the splendor of His being, for you are made in the image of the almighty, and you now have a relationship with the Father God.

2 Corinthians 10: 4 says that the weapons of our warfare are not carnal, but mighty to the pulling down of strongholds. There are other weapons that we have and instructed to use in warfare; one more is the blood of Jesus Christ. Because of the blood there is salvation and deliverance. The stripes that Jesus bore and the blood that was shed on Calvary were for our healing. 1 Peter 2:24 says, "Who his own self bare our sins in his own body on the tree that we, being dead to sins, should live unto righteousness: by whose stripes we were healed." Hebrews 10:19 says, "Having therefore boldness to enter into the holiest by the blood of Jesus."

That same blood allowed those of us who trust and are now followers, and believers of Christ Jesus to speak directly to God instead of the priest. When we plead the blood we involve the blessings that the blood stands for. This blood allows for the person filled with the Holy Ghost and baptized in the name of Jesus, to have power and dominion over the works of Satan.

In conclusion you have been commissioned to step out in faith and allow God to complete His assignment and purpose in you, your ultimate goal is to glorify God, edify His people, and further His kingdom with that same agape love that He has given to each of us.

Chapter 13

Spiritual

Gifts

Spiritual Gifts
Spiritual Gifts are spiritually discerned

1. **Helps**—The God empowered ability to assist in the needs of others.

Biblical References
1. Corinthians 12:28
2. Acts 20:35
3. 1 Thess. 5:14 support of the weak
4. Acts 6:1

Gift Traits:
1. They see what needs to be done in assisting others and they desire to do it!
2. Usually self-sacrificing and patient because of strong desire to help others.
3. They love to see others move forward in life as a result of their help.
4. They seek ways to provide relief among the poor, weak and downtrodden.
5. They like to meet immediate needs.

Gift Weaknesses:
1. They usually have difficulty saying "no" when asked to help, even when they need to say no.
2. They may wear themselves out physically and emotionally.
3. Their self worth may be too tied to their helping others.
4. They have low self-esteem
5. They make take too much ownership in their helping that they forget to let others help too.
6. They often neglect their own needs and the needs of their family to help others.

2. **Service**—The God empowered ability to meet needs in the Body of Christ and beyond, by providing the resources necessary to practically meet those needs.

Biblical References
1. Romans 12:7
2. Luke 10:38-41 Martha
3. 1 Corinthians 16:15-16
4. Romans 15: 30-31

Gift Traits:
1. They are resourceful in meeting needs
2. They offer practical solutions
3. They love to serve, often without receiving any public thanks.

4. They may find their self-esteem in doing rather than being.
5. They may get over involved and then feel abused.
6. They may use the gift to get the appreciation of others.
7. They may go around the proper authority to get the task done.
8. They have a tendency to be very pushy

3. Administration—The God empowered ability to direct the organization of the goals of the Body of Christ in such a way that plans are effectively implemented.

Biblical References
1. 1 Corinthians 12:28
2. Acts 27:11-20,27-29,38-44.
3. James 3:4 pilot steering the ship by a small rudder

Gift Traits:
1. They are very organized
2. They hear the vision and bring it into reality by putting the details of the vision (plan) into action.
3. They provide clear guidance to implement the plan or vision
4. They focus on the intimate details of the plan, rather than the big picture.
5. They are goal oriented as well as task completers.

Gift Weaknesses:
1. They often view people as "task completers" rather than people.
2. They may show favoritism to those who seem to be more loyal to them.
3. They may be unresponsive to the suggestions of others and changes in the plans that they've already made.
4. They may not communicate explanations or the process to team members.
5. They often have a hard time admitting to making mistakes.
6. They may rely on their well-organized plan of action rather than the Holy Spirit and prayer.

4. Mercy—The God empowered ability to both show great compassion and kindness to those in distresses or less fortunate, and to offer helpful and practical solutions to relieve distresses.

Biblical References;
1. Romans 12:8
2. Matthew 18:22-23
3. Matthew 20:29-34
4. Acts 9:36—Dorcas
5. Luke 10:33-35

Gift Traits:
1. They seek out ways to help the sick, poor disabled, homeless, prisoners, blind, elderly and less fortunate.
2. They show mercy in a cheerful, self-sacrificing manner.

3. They attempt to relieve the source of people's suffering
4. They feel the hurts of others and are drawn to help them.

Gift Weaknesses:
1. They may be too protective of the person(s) they are caring for.
2. They may without realizing it, identify too strongly with those who have been hurt, becoming too engulfed in the situation.
3. They can be overly emotional and base decisions solely on emotions rather than incorporating reason.
4. They may be controlled by their circumstances.
5. They may allow others to use them
6. They may not be able to set boundaries properly.

5. Giving—The God empowered ability to give freely, cheerfully, and sacrificially of one's finances or material possessions for the sake of the Body of Christ and furtherance of His Kingdom.

Biblical References:
1. Romans 12:8
2. 2 Corinthians 8:1-4 the Corinthians gave liberally,
3. Acts 4:34-37
4. Acts 5:1-10 check your motives (giving with wrong motives)
5. Ephesians 4:28 sharing with those in need.

Gift Traits:
1. They are sensitive to the financial needs of others.
2. They give freely out of the resources they have available.
3. They see finances and material possessions as tools for serving God, and set them aside for specific purposes.
4. They view giving as confidential and desire no public acknowledgement.
5. They give liberally to the church and ministries or cause which further the Kingdom of God.
6. They enjoy assuming the responsibility of meeting the financial or material needs of those in need.

Gift Weaknesses:
1. Gift projection, or judging others spirituality based on the way they do or do not give.
2. They may become lifted up in pride when much is given.
3. They may be critical of the methods of spending of others.
4. They may pressure others to give more without looking at the person's reality.
5. They may be led to give to ungodly causes
6. They often neglect the needs of their family and self in the support of ministries and their causes.

6. **Teaching**—The God empowered ability to accurately and clearly communicate biblical truths in a way that people learn, and retain what is taught.

Teaching is one of the gifts that must be developed

Biblical References:
1. Romans 12:7
2. 1 Corinthians 12:28
3. Ephesians 4:11-12 accompanies the pastoral gift here
4. Acts 18:24-28 Pricilla and Aquila more accurately explain God's way
5. Acts 5:18-21a, 25-29
6. Acts 31:1

Gift Traits:
1. They generally have a love for the Word of God
2. They have an energized hunger for studying the Word of God and are enthusiastic about teaching what they have learned.
3. They give clear biblical insight when dealing with life circumstances.
4. They enthusiastically communicate biblical truths in such a way that people readily learn and remember what was taught.
5. They are able to present clear and insightful spiritual truths with ease
6. They are able to biblically reprove, correct, encourage, and train in righteousness.

Gift Weaknesses:
1. They may appear to have all the answers, leaving little or not room for discussion.
2. They often think they have all the answers, and may be critical and impatient of others who may disagree with them.
3. They may communicate too much information for the average learner.
4. They may promote their own insight as biblical and authoritative, when functioning in their own strength, and not depending on the Holy Spirit.
5. They may be lifted up in pride because of their ability to learn and communicate biblical principles and truths.

7. **Leadership**—The God empowered ability to give vision, motivate and direct the people of God in such away that people are willing to follow their lead in accomplishing goals for the furtherance of the Kingdom of God.

If you look behind you and no one is
following, that should tell you something

Biblical References:

1. Romans 12:8
2. 1 Thess. 5:12 those over you
3. Nehemiah 4:12-22 Nehemiah is an example of a great leader
4. 1 Timothy 5:17

Gift Traits:

1. They provide oversight for the vision and direction for the overall process (the big picture).
2. They are able to see the big picture in advance.
3. They are able to effectively share the big picture with others, and involve many in the process of completing the task.
4. With diligence and zeal they take charge effectively.
5. People follow them
6. They have the ability to make decisions quickly.

Gift Weaknesses:

1. They have a tendency to be dominant and overbearing when not sensitive to the Holy Spirit
2. They often focus on authority and not ministry when operating in their own strength and not relying on the Holy Spirit to complete the task.
3. They may get caught up in the big picture and become insensitive to those carrying out the intimate details of the vision.
4. They may only see the big picture and miss the intimate details of the process of completion of the vision.

8. Martyrdom—The God empowered ability to sacrifice one's life for the cause of Christ.

Biblical References:

1. Luke 11:50-51 prophets and apostles
2. Mark 6:18-29 John the Baptist
3. Acts 7:58-60 Stephen
4. 1 Corinthians 13:3

Gift Traits:

1. They suffer for the cause of Christ with joy
2. They are very passionate about serving God even until death.
3. They will willingly die for the sake of Christ.

Gift Weaknesses:

1. Because of their passion they may suffer unnecessary by not being led by the Holy Spirit.
2. They may project this gift onto others through the use of guilt, when they are not willing to suffer as they do.

9. **Voluntary Poverty**—The God empowered ability to live in poverty in order to minister and relate to those less fortunate that they are more effectively.

This gift is not to be confused with a vow of poverty, which is a pledge to live in poverty while serving a specific mission.

Biblical References:
1. Corinthians 13:3
2. Acts 2:44-45 selling of possessions that all needs may be met
3. Acts 4:34-37

Gift Traits:
1. They set very little value on material things
2. They sacrifice all they have to minister and bring others to Christ.
3. They are very self-sacrificing.

Gift Weaknesses:
1. In their mission to reach those less fortunate, they may overextend themselves.
2. They may appear critical of those who place value on material gain.
3. They have the tendency to neglect the needs of their families.

10. **Creative Ability**—the God empowered ability to serve people and spread the Gospel of Christ through the use of the arts (music, drama, poetry, dance).

Biblical Reference;
1. 1 Chronicles 16:41-42
2. 1 Samuel 16:23
3. 2 Chronicle 5:12-14
4. Exodus 30: 22-25

Gift Traits:
1. They are very creative
2. They have a passion to serve God through what they create.
3. Their passion is to encourage through the arts (drama, music, poetry, and dance)

Gift Weaknesses:
1. They may become lifted up in pride (the I syndrome) and not give God the glory for the creations of this gift.
2. They may try to accomplish completion of the creation without relying on the Holy Spirit.

11. **Exhortation**—The God empowered ability to encourage others toward Godly living by instruction in Biblical truths, persuasive speech, or consolation and comfort.

Biblical References:
1. Romans 12: 8 to admonish console or encourage
2. Acts 2:40 to warn
3. Acts 11:22-24b encourage by Barnabus

Gift Traits:
1. They encourage others by communicating specific biblical truths and motivating practical application of scriptures.
2. They have the desire to motivate people to apply Scripture, and not just learn the Word of God.
3. They are very good at counseling others.
4. They desire to see people reach their full potential in Christ.
5. They often seek ways to uplift others.

Gift Weaknesses:
1. They often focus on the person's potential, rather than his/her reality.
2. They may have much difficulty listening to what people are actually saying before answering them.
3. They often jump to conclusion before hearing what is being said.
4. They may question the value of deep study on Christian issues and lean to the flesh or their own understanding of those issues.

12. Word of Knowledge—The God empowered ability to proclaim a message of truth through divine revelation of things learned or not known.

Biblical Reference:
1. 2 Corinthians 11:6 Paul receives spiritual insight
2. Acts 10:17-23 Peter's vision, which contained of word of knowledge.
3. Acts 16:28 Paul and the jailer

Gift Traits:
1. They speak with authority and boldness with no actual need of approval from people.
2. Words or phrases often appear in their mind
3. They are unusually sensitive to the Holy Spirit
4. They are very confident about what has been revealed to them.

Gift Weaknesses:
1. They may not listen to the Holy Spirit fully and share a word of knowledge at the wrong time or place causing confusion, or someone to stray in the wrong direction.
2. They may not fully rely on the Holy Spirit and relay a message that has not been given by God out of self.
3. They may become prideful because of their biblical insight, and the messages that are divinely revealed.
4. They may appear very opinionated and dogmatic.

13. Word of Wisdom—The God empowered ability to proclaim and apply Godly principles to the circumstances of a given task.

Biblical References:
1. Luke 21:14-15 Irrefutable wisdom
2. Col. 1:26-227 God's wisdom revealed
3. 1 Corinthians 12:8
4. 2 Peter 3:15-16a Paul wrote with wisdom

Gift Traits:
1. They have an impeccable understanding of Biblical truths.
2. They have the ability to reveal the will of God in situations that they had not previous knowledge.
3. They offer practical, solutions to problems.
4. They are unusually sensitive to the Holy Spirit.
5. They speak with authority

Gift Weaknesses:
1. They may become prideful once they realize that people actually listen to them. And give their own wisdom instead of God's resulting in an ineffective answer.
2. They may become overzealous and speak out of term when God has not spoken at all.
3. They may become impatient with people who don't carry out the word of wisdom that was given.

14. Prophecy—The God empowered ability to reveal divine messages of God declaring futuristic or present truths evoking understanding, correction, repentance, or edification.

Biblical References:
1. Acts 2:17
2. 1 Corinthians 13:24-25
3. 2 Chronicles 9:3, 17, 18, 23
4. Acts 21:8-11
5. Ephesians 4:11

Gift Traits:
1. They receive and reveal the mind of God
2. They enjoy public speaking (this does not mean that all public speakers are prophetic).
3. They speak with authority and conviction.
4. They are very sensitive to the Holy Spirit and it's prompting.
5. They are intercessors (although they may not claim to be)

Gift Weaknesses:

1. Because of their eagerness, they may speak forth prophecy this is not in line with God's word.
2. They may be impatient and judgmental.
3. In their eagerness, they may try to convict rather than relying on the Holy Spirit to do the convicting.
4. At times they may be blunt and condemning
5. They may become prideful, when they realize that people will listen to them.
6. They may at times out of fear not give the message of God has given.

There are three categories of prophesy, and not all prophetic calls are alike in their operation, as each person is unique in their gifting, gift mix and abilities.

    a) *Personal Prophecy* is the delivering of a prophetic word from God to an individual, revealing the secrets of the heart so that the individual, understands, repents or is edified.

    b) *Corporate Prophecy* is the delivering of a prophetic word to a body or congregation of believers.

    c) *Prophetic Intercession* is the ability to pray and intercede with prophetic insight and for specific issues as God empowers them to do so.

People with the prophetic gift often pray differently from other people, as this one of the first ways that those with this gift receive what they later come to realize has been a prophetic word. God uses intercession as the training ground for this gift. God through the prompting and power of the Holy Spirit inspires these intercessors to pray beyond their natural knowledge, and these people often find themselves in hot water for praying about things that they should have no knowledge of, especially in churches where traditionally there is no understanding of the prophetic gift.

Understand that not all intercessors are prophetic, but all prophets are intercessors. These intercessors often stand in the gap as a defender for people, cause and nations. (Gen. 18)

Prophetic intercessors are often stretched and receive very rigorous and demanding training regardless of their call or purpose.

The primary goal of the prophet or those with the gift of prophecy is to help the person or congregation whichever, to receive the prophetic word from God who sent the word in the first place, being careful of their approach and style, to communicate that word in such a way that the receiver will be edified. The prophet or prophetic gift bearer must also be open to correction by the body of Christ, or the pastor of the local church, as all prophecy must be in line with the word of God, and what is happening in that particular body.

A thought to remember: *"Every tree is known by the fruit it bears". Check out the fruit. (Matthew 7:15-18, 20)*

15. Miracles—The God empowered ability to manifest divine intervention in extraordinary events or human affairs that cannot be explained by natural law.

Biblical References:
1. John 11:38-44 the dead raised
2. Exodus 17:1-7
3. John 2:1-11 Jesus turned water into wine

Gift Traits:
1. God uses as them as a vessel to perform supernatural acts.
2. They move with authority and boldness in their faith.
3. They believe God with extraordinary confidence
4. Other people confirm the manifestation of these supernatural acts.
5. They believe with certainty that God can move mountain without wavering in their faith.

Gift Weaknesses:
1. They may attempt to produce miracles without relying on God to do the miraculous.
2. They may claim to have performed miracles, but there is no confirmation that it ever happened.
3. They may become lifted up in pride and develop the I syndrome, in not given the glory to God for this benefit.
4. They may feel responsible when a miracle does not happen.

16. Faith—The God empowered ability to trust and believe that God is able to perform every promise, and work out His purpose in every situation.

Biblical References:
1. Hebrews 11 chapter that refers to faith
2. Romans 4:20 unwavering faith
3. 1 Corinthians 12:9
4. Acts 6:5-8
5. Acts 11:24
6. Mark 5:27-28, 34 the hemorrhaging woman

Gift Traits:
1. They believe that God is able to do the impossible
2. They are willing to seek and yield to God's will rather than waiver or question his ability to perform the impossible.
3. They step out in faith when others are not so willing to do so.
4. They take God at His word literally.

Gift Weaknesses:
1. They have tendencies at times to exercise their faith without love.
2. They may set others up for failure, because of their blind faith.
3. They may have the tendency to project this gift onto others.
4. They may become impatient with others who don't have this gift.

*Each of us has a measure of faith,
God's word says, we only need mustard seed faith*

17. Healings—The God empowered ability that God gives to certain members of the Body of Christ to restore people to health in the physical, emotional or spiritual areas.

There are many gifts of healings according 1 Corinthians 12: 9. Therefore there is no specific method that one may be used in the operation of these gifts. We are used as God's instrument to bring about restoration of health as He chooses.

Biblical References:
1. 1 Corinthians 12:9
2. Luke 5: 17-20 physical and spiritual healing
3. Luke 8:26-32 demon possessed man healed

Gift Traits
1. The gift of faith often accompanies this gift, as the bearer of this gift believes that God can heal every infirmity whether physical, emotional, or spiritual.
2. Because they realize that they are the vessel that God uses to heal, they are willing to pray for the healing of all who seek it, understanding that is God's will to heal or not at that time, and that there may be a bigger picture for glorification of God.
3. They are sensitive and often relate well with those who suffer.

Gift Weaknesses:
1. They may often be lead to neglect medical resources, because of their emphasis on the healing power of God.
2. They may become lifted up in pride and fall into the I syndrome, and seek personal gain in the use of this gift.
3. To protect their reputation may resort to unethical practices in the use of this gift, by exaggerating claims of healings that actually aren't proven to be true.
4. They may feel that they have failed when God chooses not to heal.

18. Celibacy—The God empowered ability to commit oneself wholeheartedly to the work of and service of God by remaining single.

*Not to be confused with the grace of celibacy,
as we all are to remain celibate until marriage,
but do have thoughts of marriage at some point in
life. Also not to be confused with celibacy derived
from hurt or anger from one of the opposite sex.*

Biblical References:
1. 1 Corinthians 7:7—Paul and the gift of celibacy
2. 1 Corinthians 7:32-35

Gift Traits:
1. They enjoy being single and have no desire to be married.
2. They spend a great deal of time in serving God wholeheartedly using this and their other gifts.
3. They have knowledge of and understand God's will for their life.
4. They desire to commit all of their time to serving God in ministry.

Gift Weaknesses:
1. They may often feel guilty because of their desire to be single.
2. They may become loners
3. They may find themselves being pressured into marriage by others, and do so just to please them, resulting in devastation.

19. **Intercession**—The God empowered ability to pray for long periods of time on the behalf of people, causes, nations, etc. as the Holy Spirit gives the unction.

Intercessors flow in this gift in two categories.

   a) *Intercessory Prayers*—Those that are simply unctioned to pray for long periods of time for others as the Holy Spirit gives the unction or when asked to pray by those in need of prayer.
   b) *Prophetic Intercessors*—Those called as watchmen for the Body of Christ. These fall into three sub-categories.

   1. *The Jeremiah Watchman*—Unctioned to verbally declare God's will for a particular situation.
   2. *The Harvest Watchman*—Those unctioned to watch or oversee in prayer the harvest fields of the Body of Christ from the nursery to senior citizens, for new converts, and those who interact with them.
   3. *The Warrior Watchman*—Those unctioned to actively engage in the act of prophetic intercession, sound the alarm, militantly, stand against the enemy (Satan) and stand in the gap for those within the Body of Christ.

Biblical References:
1. James 5:16—The effectual fervent prayers of the righteous man
2. Luke 2:36-38—Anna and intercession
3. Colossians 1:9-12

Gift Traits:
1. They enjoy praying for others.
2. They often respond to the need of prayer for others quickly.
3. They often experience being awakened in the middle of the night with urgency to pray.
4. They often receive and urgently pray for people, causes, or nations.

Gift Weaknesses:

1. They often neglect their own personal needs and health because of he urgency they feel to pray.
2. They may appear overly forceful during prayer, which can frighten, or distract others during corporate prayer meetings.
3. They may acquire a competitive spirit during prayer as to who can pray the loudest, often disturbing others during prayer (its not how loud one prays but the fervency of the prayer that counts).

20. Tongues—The God empowered ability that God gives to certain members of the Body of Christ to speak to God in a language not learned by the bearer for the edification of self and to receive and communicate an immediate message of God to His people through a divine utterance not learned or known by the bearer.

Biblical References:

1. Acts 2: 1-13—tongues of fire, other tongues as the Spirit gives utterance.
2. Acts 10: 44-46 Holy Spirit fell upon those who heard the word.
3. Acts 19: 1-7

There are two categories of the gifts of tongues:

1. *Spiritual Prayer Language*, whereby one edifies him/herself in prayer and praise. This tongue is directed from the bearer to God and needs no interpretation. (1 Corinthians 2, 4: 16-17)
2. *Corporate tongues* which in an immediate message from God to His people in a divine utterance to edify the people of Go. This tongue requires and must be interpreted. (1 Corinthians 14: 26-28)

Gift Traits:

1. They usually have a very strong and stable prayer life.
2. They do not always know what they are saying.
3. They see prayer a relational rather than asking God.
4. In corporate tongues, they have a clear sense of receiving a message from God.
5. They speak with authority.

Gift Weaknesses:

1. They may become lifted up in pride and think that they are better or more spiritual than those who do not have this gift.
2. They may feel this gift is more important than the actual evidences of Christian character as Fruit of the Spirit, etc.
3. This gift cannot be taught to others, it is not a learned language.
4. They may not use this gift in love, which will cause discord rather than unity within the body.
5. They may be tempted to project this gift on others.

21. Interpretation of Tongues—The God empowered ability to receive, interpret and communicate an immediate message from God given by one spoken in tongues.

Biblical References:
1. 1 Corinthians 12:10
2. 1 Corinthians 14:5
3. 1 Corinthians 14: 27-28

Interpretation of tongues strengthens and
comforts the Body of Christ.

Gift Traits:
1. They have a clear sense of receiving an interpretation of a message spoken in corporate tongues.
2. They speak with authority

Gift Weaknesses:
1. They have a tendency to try to explain the messages, which come from God instead of the interpretation alone.
2. They may become lifted up in pride when they realize that people really listen to them.
3. In the eagerness to interpret the message of tongues, they may give a message that was not inspired by God, or given by Him.

22. **Discernment of Spirits**—The God empowered ability to discern the source (God, self, or Satan) of an action or behavior.

Discernment of spirits is not to be confused
with discernment of truth and error, or differentiating
between right and wrong, which each of us has,
and must choose to put it to use.

Biblical Reference:
1. 1 Corinthians 12:10
2. 2 Corinthians 11:13-15 the necessity of discernment of spirits.
3. 1 John 4: 1-3 testing the spirits to see if they are of God
4. Ephesians 6:12

Gift Traits:
1. They have the ability to assist others identifying the root of their spiritual problems.
2. They are quick to analyze people and situations for their spiritual pulse.
3. They are able to discern the true spiritual motivation of people.
4. They can often see in the spirit realm and distinguish the strongholds of an area or person.

Gift Weaknesses:
1. They may become overzealous and seek to find demons, principalities, and call all behaviors as being caused by the demonic.
2. They may be judgmental of others and their motives.

3. They may be impatient with the process of real change in that person's situation or life.

23. Exorcism—The God empowered ability to expel or cast out demons.

We all in the Body of Christ are called
to cast out demons, which is one of
the things that the Word of God
says will follow us. Evil
spirits cannot be counseled
They must be cast out.

Biblical References:
1. Acts 8:5-8 Philip preaches and spirits leave
2. Acts 19: 13-16 Paul and the sons of Sceva
3. Mark 5: 1-13 Jesus and the demon processed woman

Gift Traits:
1. This gift is accompanied by the gift of discernment of spirits.
2. They approach casting our demons boldness.
3. They are acquainted with the spirit world and demonic strategies.
4. They have a strong and stable prayer life.
5. They understand the authority of the name of Jesus.

Gift Weaknesses:
1. They may neglect to distinguish between psychological disorders, and the demon possessed.
2. In their seeking of demons to cast out, they may attribute every behavior as demons.
3. They may not ask for help when needed in areas of deliverance.
4. They may become impatient with people who choose to still walk in bondage or oppression after being prayed for.
5. They may have the tendency to neglect their own physical and emotional health or well-being.

Because of the transference of the demonic,
if you are new or just found out that you
have this gift, it is my suggestion that you
work with someone else who is well
developed in this gift, as you develop this gift.

24. Pastoring—The God empowered ability to oversee, care for and nurture individuals or groups of individuals in the Body of Christ toward spiritual maturity on a long-term basis.

Biblical References:
1. Ephesians 4: 11-12—gifts to the Body of Christ
2. John 21: 16—Peter called to feed God's sheep
3. Ezekiel 34—shepherd and sheep

Gift Traits:
1. They have a strong desire to see people learn and grow into spiritual maturity for the long haul.
2. They are usually known as the nurturers of the Body of Christ.
3. They seek to spiritually build up people in biblical truths.
4. They usually counsel and guide many individuals through biblical principles.

Gift weaknesses:
1. They may become overly sensitive to the needs of people and not be able to make hard decisions.
2. They have tendencies to neglect the nurturing of their immediate families.
3. They may try to control people's decisions by use of guilt.
4. They may have problems with those who leave their church, and go to another church out of jealousy, or sense of failure.

25. **Apostle**—The God empowered ability to evangelize and build foundations for new churches and works of ministry to enhance the spread of the Gospel.

Biblical References:
1. Ephesians 4: 11-12
2. 1 Corinthians 12:28
3. Romans 15:14-21—Paul laying a foundation for the spread of the gospel
4. Acts 114:14—Paul and Barnabus as apostles

Gift Traits:
1. They build foundations by preaching the gospel to the unsaved and organize and equip the saints to do the work of ministry.
2. They speak with authority and people respond with enthusiasm by becoming saved and doing the work of ministry.
3. They enjoy starting new works of ministry
4. They are able to organize a new work of ministry or church effectively for Christ and the spread of the Gospel.

Gift Weaknesses:
1. They may move to the next foundation before adequately securing the foundation that is at hand.
2. They may through pride (the I syndrome) not give the credit of the new foundation to God.
3. They may not be sensitive to the Holy Spirit's lead and rely on their own strength to build foundations or new churches.
4. They may target people to complete the task at hand without being sensitive to their on going needs.

26. **Missionary**—The God empowered ability to use his/her spiritual gifts to minister or serve in another culture.

Biblical Reference:
1. Acts 13:2—Barnabas and Saul sent away to do work of ministry
2. Romans 10:13-15
3. 1 Corinthians 9:19-23 serving all, as to win more to Christ

Gift Traits:
1. They love to travel and often live out of a suitcase.
2. They are moved by the needs of others and seek ways to relieve them while proclaiming the Gospel.
3. They enjoy living in and learning first hand about other cultures.

Gift Weaknesses:
1. They often become engulfed with the needs of others and neglect their own and family needs.
2. They may feel insecure at first about using their gifts in another culture.
3. They may focus on their traveling and learning more than the work of ministry.

27. Evangelism—The God empowered ability to share the gospel with non-believers and those who have not heard the gospel in such a way that they respond and become followers of Christ.

Not to be confused with revivalist, which is one who travels and revives the Saints in many areas with the gospel.

Bible References:
1. Ephesians 4:11-12
2. Acts 8:26-37
3. 2 Timothy 4:5—fulfillment of ministry by doing the work of an evangelist.

Gift Traits:
1. They have a strong desire to share the gospel and their faith with all people.
2. They speak with authority and boldness.
3. They communicate the gospel in such conviction that it is clearly understood and the hearer responds.
4. They are able to relay the plan of salvation both scripturally and practically that it causes a response.

Gift Weaknesses:
1. They often see people as targets and may not be sensitive to their reality.
2. They may often use guilt as a motivator to persuade people to accept Christ.
3. They can often be overbearing in their approach.
4. They may become lifted up in pride with the number of those responding to the plan of salvation. (The I syndrome)

Hospitality—The God empowered ability to open one's home (also church home) to strangers and guest, making them feel comfortable and welcome.

Biblical References:
1. Hebrew 13: 1-2
2. Romans 16: 23
3. Acts 18: 24-26
4. 1 Corinthians 16:19

Gift Traits:
1. They enjoy meeting people, and often meet no strangers.
2. They desire to provide lodging, food and companionship to strangers and guest in need.
3. They often neglect the needs of themselves and their family to secure the comfort of others.

Gift Weaknesses:
1. They may at times extend their desire to comfort and meet needs to the wrong persons.
2. They have difficulty in saying no, when necessary.
3. They may put down others when they do not have the same concerns about people as they do.

Review

1. Who has been given Spiritual Gifts (1 Cor.2: 12-14)?

2. Every Christian has at least _____ gift.
    (1 Peter 4: 10)

3. According to 1 Corinthians 12:29-30, does everybody have the same gift?

4. How do you earn your spiritual gift? (Eph. 4: 7)

5. Can you lose you spiritual gifts if you don't use it? (Romans 11:29)

6. I should not _____ my gift but I should _____ it. (1Timothy 4:14)

7. I am to be a good _____ over the gifts God has given me. (1 Cor. 4:1-2, Matthew 25:14-40)

8. I should use my gift to _____ others. (1 Peter 4:10)

9. If I don't use my gift in _____ it is of no avail.
    (1 cor.13: 1)

10. When I use my gift I _____ God. (1 Peter 4:11)

11. In your own words explain verse 2 of Romans 12:1-8.

12. What do verses 1 and 2 in Romans 12 have to do with understanding and operating in our spiritual gifts?

13. According to verse 3 in Romans 13, how should we think of ourselves? Why should we think of ourselves in this manner?

14. According to Romans 12, how does the Body of Christ function like the human body?

15. The phrase "according to the grace given." is repeated at least twice in the 12th chapter of Romans. What does grace have to do with spiritual gifts?

16. What spiritual gifts are listed in verses 6-8 of Romans 12 and how are we to use each gift?

1.	6.	11.
2.	7.	12.
3.	8.	13.
4.	9.	
5.	10.	

17. There are two responses to the call of God on your life. What are they? And what do they result in?

18. Name four foundational barriers that hinder people from saying, "yes" to God's call or purpose.

19. Give one scripture to counteract these foundational barriers.

1.

2.

3.

4.

20. Why are Spiritual Gifts given?

21. What is the definition of a Spiritual Gift?

22. List the eight qualities of a servant.

                         1.   5.
                         2.   6.
                         3.   7.
                         4.   8.

23. Are all intercessors prophets?

24. According to 1 Corinthians 12:29-30, does everybody have the same Spiritual Gift?

25. After becoming a Christian there are four areas of your life that will began to change. What are they?

1.
2.
3.
4.

26. Why does God give us a passion?

27. What is the difference in a talent and a Spiritual Gift?

28. There are many schools of thought on purpose, passion,
Spiritual gifts, and serving within the Body of Christ. What are the views of your pastor or overseer?

29. God has given us armor and weapons of warfare. What are they?

30. What are our defensive weapons of warfare?

Bibliographical References

The Voice of God
Cindy Jacobs
Regal Books 1995

Your Spiritual Gifts Can Help Your Church
C. Peter Wagner
Regal Books 1979

In Pursuit of Purpose
Myles Monroe
Destiny Image Publishers 1992

What You Do Best In The Body Of Christ
Bruce Bugbee
Zondervan Publishing House 1974

How to Forgive When It's Hard to Forget
Joy Haney
New Leaf Press 1995

Scripture Quotations—Holy Bible
New King James Version—Thomas Nelson Publisher—1979, 1980
New International Version—Zondervan Publishing House—1973, 1978, 1984

A Woman's Guide to Spirit Filled Living
Quin Sherrer & Ruthanne Garlode
Servant Publications 1996

Knowledge of the Holy
A.W. Tozer
Harper Collins Publishers 1961